A= _____

B= _____

C= _____

Also by Wilson L. Triviño, Ph.D.

Remember your ABCs: *A simple guide on how to become a success and live the life YOU want to lead!*

Remember your ABCs Lite: quotes and ideas that will empower you to live the life YOU want to lead!

Remember Your

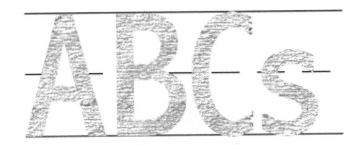

Quotes and ideas that will empower you
to live the life YOU want to lead!

Wilson L. Triviño, Ph.D.
C. David Triviño

Aura Free Press
Marietta, GA

6

Aura Free Press
379 Pat Mell Road, Ste. 814
Marietta, GA 30060

First Edition
Copyright @ 2003

Cover Design and Text Layout:
Miguel A. Triviño
T4 Associates

ISBN Number: 0-9743226-1-X

DEDICATION

To all of our teachers at the Marietta City and
Cobb County School System that gave us the
gift of reading. This gift open our minds to
a world of knowledge and opportunity. Their
high expectations and support in our dreams
have lead to our successes. These selfless
public servants do touch the future by teaching.

CONTENTS

First say to yourself what you would be and then do what you have to do.
~Ralph Waldo Emerson

I do not think there is any other quality so essential to success of any kind as the quality of perseverance.
~John D. Rockefeller

Coming together is a beginning;
Keeping together is progress,
Working together is success.
~Henry Ford

You miss 100 percent of the shots you never take.
~Wayne Gretzky

The story of the human race is men and women selling themselves short.
~Abraham Maslow

PREFACE

Wilson L. Triviño, Ph.D.

L ife is an adventure! All of us struggle each day. In *Remember Your ABCs*, I simplified the ideas that have made successful individuals realize their dreams. In this book, *Remember Your ABCs Lite* edition I attempt to capture the antidotal observations from my years of research of the world's top thinkers and achievers. The three basic principles of success, which are your Attitude, Beliefs, and Commitment, serve as the beginning of your journey toward your dreams. The ABC method was created to help capture the wisdom of the ages. The most challenging part of this simple method is to focus on applying these principles each and every day.

This work is also a collaborated effort with my motivator and brother, David Triviño. David is a successful entrepreneur who brings a practical approach to success.

I hope that you will enjoy the book and continue to live the life YOU want to lead!

A= Attitude

B= Beliefs

C= Commitment

Our life is but a grain of sand in the oceans,
and but a second in time.
Don't get caught up in working for the
future that you forget to live today.
Take the time to notice and enjoy the
small things of today, because eventually
today will become tomorrow and will
be remembered as yesterday.
~Anonymous

If you ever have it under control, you
aren't really racing.
~Mario Andretti

INTRODUCTION

A B C s

Success is living the life YOU want to lead!
~Wilson L.Triviño, Ph.D.
www.abcvision.us

Remember Your ABCs!

Attitude= Vision~ Where do I want to go?

    1- Acceptance

    2- Assess

    3- Action

Beliefs= Core Values~ Why do I want to do this?

    1- Break from the past

    2- Begin

    3- Believe

Commitment= Focus~ How will I get there?

    1- Continual change

    2- Clear Vision

    3- Continue the Journey

SUCCESS is FOREVER!

~Stanley Williams

Introduction
By David and Wilson Triviño

Regardless of your race, gender, or philosophy, all of us want to be happy everyday. We have good days, we have bad days. The days turn into months, which turn into years and evolve into a lifetime. If we don't take charge of our thoughts and actions today, then we will miss an opportunity. Remind yourself that today, is the tomorrow we worried about yesterday.

We attempt to create our vision and develop a strategy to implement these goals. Unfortunately, some times we tend to forget the basics. The ABC concept captures the best ideas that allow everyone to refocus. By spelling out our dreams and creating a road map, we will more likely reach our destination, rather than simply being lost in motion. The three forces that will empower your destiny center around your Attitude, Beliefs, and Commitment.

The basic outline of this book is simple, each chapter is divided into subject areas. This book should be used as a reference and reviewed daily. We live in a time of information overload. We have the internet, television, and noise thrown at us in this 24 hour cycle world. Most of us allocate time for our physical health, by eating and exercising, our social health, by being with our friends, and family, our financial health, by saving for our retirement and paying our bills; however we tend not to spend time on our mental health, our mental outlook is probably the most important aspect of our daily lives. If we do not take the time to refocus and filter out the noise, we will drown with information. The world is starving for wisdom and practical advice. This book will serve as a simple method to pick up and review ideas from the world's leaders and achievers.

The first chapter addresses the core of any successful individual and that is Attitude. Your attitude is the mental outlook that shapes your perception of reality. You choose what you become. Destiny is achieved either consciously or unconsciously, and you determine your fate. By being conscious of your attitude, you can become more open to new possibilities. The person you are today is a result of all the decisions you have made up to this point in your life. Whatever the mind of an individual can conceive, they can achieve. You alone bear the responsibility of shaping your own destiny.

The second chapter centers on your Beliefs. Regardless of whether you are conscious of it or not, you make all the decisions in your life based on your beliefs. Your beliefs are the congruent internal representation that governs your behavior. They are formed as a result of the sum of your experiences throughout your life so far and have created the foundation on which you stand, determining what you can or can't do. This chapter will enable you to re-examine your beliefs and become conscious of how they guide you each day. In this chapter, you need to first break free from the past and understand the limitations it creates. Begin the process and believe in challenging yourself and answering the right questions. Then consciously you will discover the awesome potential that lies within you.

The next chapter is the most crucial in realizing your dreams that of Commitment. You need to stay the course and realize that life is not a sprint, it is a marathon. Our youngest brother, Daniel, ran his first marathon in San Diego, California. Twenty six miles of stamina, sweat, and determination. Once finished, we congratulated him, we asked him how did he finish? His response was simple, "I just ran one step at a time, even when I wanted to slow down and walk, I told myself to stay the course". What an awesome observation! You have to stick it out through the bad times as well as the good. No one said that living your dreams was going to be easy. It is tough, but so are you.

We are all leaders. This next chapter focuses on Leadership. In taking charge of our Attitude, Beliefs, and Commitment, we need to also take on challenges. By awakening the leader within, we create a new path and determine our destiny.

Of course, being presidential scholars we had to include a chapter on Presidential Wisdom. We were very fortunate to be invited to the 100 year anniversary of the West Wing of the White House and be given a tour by the President. We have visited 9 of the 10 Presidential libraries. This chapter is devoted to the ideas from our nation's chief executives.

Finally, not to take ourselves too seriously, we have included a chapter on Humor. Life is a journey, and we need to enjoy it. Why not laugh along the way and smile.

We hope that you will enjoy the ideas found within this book and if you have a good quote to share for future editions, please send it to us.

Focus on today, because yesterday is gone, tomorrow it not guaranteed and today is a gift from the present. Control your destiny or someone else will. *Remember Your ABCs* and become a SUCCESS by living the life YOU want to lead!

ONE

A is for Attitude

The action is gone, all we got are the results
~C. David Triviño

You can conquer almost any fear if you will only make up your mind to do so. For remember, fear doesn't exist anywhere except in the mind.
~Dale Carnegie

Everything can be taken from a man except the last of human freedoms— to choose one's attitude in any given set of circumstances.
~Vicktor E. Frankl

Remember the 5 simple rules to be happy:
1. Free your heart from hatred.
2. Free your mind from worries.
3. Live simply.
4. Give more.
5. Expect less.

What determines the path your life will take is your reaction to life's experiences. Your attitude influences how you interact with the world around you, either positively or negatively. Each day is a series of decisions about life's journey. A clear and positive mental attitude enables us to think from the perspective of possibility rather than seeing only the limitations.

We have two futures in front of us: the one that we drift into or the one that we choose. Why not go after the future you choose and live your dreams! The quotes in this chapter will explore some of the components of a healthy attitude and how you can shape it.

You have a very powerful mind that can make anything happen as long as you keep yourself centered.
~Dr. Wayne W. Dyer

Cream doesn't rise to the top, it works its way up.
~Harvey Mackay

When the student is ready, the teacher will appear.
~Zen

If you have a problem, do 3 things:

1- Ask yourself, "What is the worst that can possibly happen?"
2- Prepare to accept if you have to.
3- Then calmly proceed to improve on the worst.
~Dale Carnegie

Success is the progressive realization of a worthy ideal.
~Earl Nightingale

Whether you think you can or whether you think you can't, you're right!
~Henry Ford

Our experiences and feelings are mainly related to our bodies and our minds. We know from our daily experience that mental happiness is beneficial. For instance, two people may face the same kind of tragedy, one person may face it more easily than the other due to his or her mental attitude.
~His Holiness the XIV Dalai Lama

HOW TO DEAL WITH PROBLEMS

Here is how I do it. I enter my library, close my eyes, and walk to certain shelves containing only books on history. With my eyes shut, I reach for a book, not knowing whether I am picking up Prescott's Conquest of Mexico or Suetonius lives of the Twelve Ceasars. With my eyes still closed, I open the book at random. I then open my eyes and read for an hour; and the more I read, the more sharply I realize that the world has always been in the throes of agony, that civilization has always been tottering on the brink. The pages of history fairly shriek with tragic tales of war, famine, poverty, pestilence, and man's inhumanity to man. After reading history for an hour, I realize that as bad as conditions are now, they are infinitely better than they used to be. This enables me to see and face my present troubles in their proper perspective as well as to realize that the world as a whole is constantly growing better.
~Roger W. Babson

Take a moment now to envision what you really want in your life.

1.

2.

3.

4.

5.

If you don't know where you are going you will end up someplace else.

~Vicky K. Hood

The following story shows how constant self-improvement is necessary. There was a man on his way to work and he observed a lumberjack sawing a big old oak tree. Later in that day, he then again saw this logger moving his whole body back and forth with his saw focusing all his energies into knocking down this huge old tree. He noticed the sun burnt face and sweat stained shirt that reflected his tireless efforts. Wanting to help, the man stopped and asked the lumber jack cutting down, "Why have you not taken a break? Would it not make sense to stop, rest, and sharpen your saw? It would make your work much easier." The lumber jack did not take this suggestion very well and harshly responded, "You don't know anything about cutting trees, besides I don't have time to waste on taking a break, I need to cut it down now!"

Now I ask you, have you taken time out to sharpen your saw? Have you focused on where you want to go? Do you realize that the purpose of life is to have a life's purpose. The time to plan the next twenty years is today, not twenty years from now.

~Steven Covey

Ask yourself, "Where am I at this stage in my life?" Examine your physical, spiritual, social, financial, and professional roles and how you stand. Are you totally satisfied? Be honest and remember, once you take responsibilities, you can free yourself up to do something about it. List them now:

Physical:

Spiritual:

Social:

Financial:

Professional

Senator Max Cleland's
Rules to live to the MAX!

1. Life is a Daring Adventure
2. Risk Changing
3. Prepare Yourself to Win
4. You Gotta Believe
5. Turn Your Scars into Stars
6. Think Positively
7. Reach for the Sky
8. Press on!
9. Let God work out things
10. Success is a team effort
11. Be of good courage
12. Enjoy all things

If you can conceive it and believe it, you will achieve it.
~Napolean Hill

Don't let the mistakes and disappointments of the past direct and control your future.
~Zig Ziglar

Here is a quick mental exercise to show you the power of attitude. Take the word ATTITUDE and count the location of each letter of the word in the alphabet. For instance, A is number one, T is number 18 and so forth. If you add the location of each word up, they equal 100!! This shows that attitude is already 100 percent of your focus.

When everything seems to be going against you, remember that the airplane takes off against the wind, not with it.
~Henry Ford

Life is either a daring adventure or nothing.
~Helen Keller

If you don't run your own life, somebody else will.
~John Atkinson

Our greatest glory is not in never falling, but in rising every time we fall.
~Confucious

Destiny is not a matter of chance, it is a matter of choice; it is not to be waited for, it is a thing to be achieved.
~Williams Jennings Bryan

Listen to the spirit within, it is your natural protective hedge.
~"General" Hafeezah

There are two things to aim at in life;
first to get what you want; and after
that, to enjoy it. Only the wisest of
mankind achieve the second.
~Logan Pearsall Smith

Positive thinking is realistic thinking.
It always sees the negative, but it
doesn't dwell on the negative and
nurture it, letting it dominate the
mind. It keeps the negative in proper
size, and grows the positive big.
Thus, it enables countless men and
women to have serenity and power-
despite continuing pain.
~Dr. Norman Vincent Peale

No one can go back and make a brand
new start. Anyone can start from now
and make a brand new ending.
~Unknown

Kiwanis International

The six permanent Objects of Kiwanis International were approved by Kiwanis club delegates at the 1924 Convention in Denver, Colorado. Through the succeeding decades, they have remained unchanged.

1.To give primacy to the human and spiritual rather than to the material values of life.

2. To encourage the daily living of the Golden Rule in all human relationships.

3.To promote the adoption and the application of higher social, business, and professional standards.

4.To develop, by precept and example, a more intelligent, aggressive, and serviceable citizenship.

5.To provide, through Kiwanis clubs, a practical means to form enduring friendships, to render altruistic service, and to build better communities.

6.To cooperate in creating and maintaining that sound public opinion and high idealism which make possible the increase of righteousness, justice, patriotism, and goodwill.

The name "Kiwanis" was adapted from the expression "Nunc Kee-wanis" in the Otchipew (Native American) language, meaning "We have a good time," "We make a noise," or, under another construction, "We trade or advertise." Some persons prefer to pronounce the word "ki"; others, "kee."

TWO

B is for Beliefs

Life is a game...Are you winning?
~John Cooper
www.createawonderfullife.com

One Person Can Make a Difference

One song can spark a memory
One flower can waken a dream,
One tree can start a forest,
One bird can herald spring,
One smile can start a friendship,
One handclasp can lift a soul.
One star can guide a ship at sea,
One speech can set a goal.
One vote can change a nation,
One sunbeam can light a room.
One candle can erase the darkness,
One laugh can chase the gloom.
One step must start each journey,
One word must start each prayer.
One hope can raise the spirits,
One prayer can show you care.
One can make a difference. YOU CAN!

~Charles Gould

~Given to the authors by the
Honorable Gresham Howren

Your beliefs are best defined as the congruent internal representation that governs behavior. What creates beliefs? Five specific factors define your belief system. They are your environment, events in your life, knowledge, past results, and goals. If you live in poverty, filled with despair, then you will believe that the world lacks hope. If you grow up in an environment like the one I had, with entrepreneurial parents and positive support, then you believe in opportunity over adversity.

The events in your life also shape your view. If you have witnessed success, you will be more likely to reach for success. Knowledge is also an important key to a winning belief system. An education makes you realize that the more you learn the less you know and opens your mind's eye to a world of possibility. That is why continuous learning is a must for continuous success.

Past results determine your fate: if you have been successful throughout your life, you will feel that you can reach for success.

If you have always deemed your actions a failure, then you will fail in your actions. Finally, and probably the most important factor in your belief system, examine your goals. If you have a vision and know what you want from life, you will reach beyond your grasp and push yourself to the outer limits. Seek and you shall receive.

A woman is like a teabag. You don't
know her strength until she is in hot
water.
~Nancy Reagan

Whoever gossips will gossip about
you.
~Spanish Proverb

Give love and unconditional
acceptance to those you encounter,
and notice what happens.
~Dr. Wayne W. Dyer

Do you remember the things you were
worrying about a year ago? How did
they work out? Didn't you waste a lot
of fruitless energy on account of most
of them? Didn't most of them turn
out all right after all?
~Dale Carnegie

The greatest glory of living lies not in never falling, but in rising every time you fall.
~Nelson Mandela

When you lie down with dogs, you can't be shocked to get fleas. When you lie down with a wolf, you must count yourself lucky to come out with you jugular intact.
~Sarah Ferguson- Dutches of York

The only people who have the easy answers are the people who don't have responsibilities.
~Clarence J. Thomas
U.S. Supreme Court Justice

A man's character is his fate.
~Heracleitus

Man is the only animal that blushes or
needs to.
~Mark Twain

Your belief determines your action
and your action determines your
results, but first you have to believe.
~Mark Victor Hansen

It is this belief in a power larger than
myself and other than myself which
allows me to venture into the
unknown and even the unknowable.
~Maya Angelou

The environment you fashion out of
your thoughts, your beliefs, your
ideals, your philosophy is the only
climate you will ever live in. The key
is in not spending time, but in
investing it.
~Stephen R. Covey

What on earth would a man do with himself if something didn't stand in his way?
~H.G. Wells

The Secret to life is in art.
~Oscar Wilde, author

Follow the Path of others to Success. Learn from other to make up for your lack of experience in any way. Be receptive to people around you. They have things to teach you. Take advantage of the people that have made the journey ahead of you.

Try to pick the right role models. Don't look for people that make you feel good or entertain you. Look for people that can help you.

Role models are more than people you like and admire. The key is to look for people that will help you be more successful. You can learn from the mistakes of others. You can learn different approaches overcoming challenges. Learning what not to do is sometimes as important as learning what to do. Success depends on using not opposing.
~ABC Vision

Phenomenal Woman
Maya Angelo

Pretty women wonder where my secret lies.
I'm not cute or built to suit
a fashion model's size
But when I start to tell them,
they think I'm telling lies.
I say, It's in the reach of my arms,
The span of my hips,
The stride of my step,
The curl of my lips.
I'm a woman
Phenomenally.
Phenomenal woman,
That's me.
I walk into a room
Just as cool as you please,
And to a man,
The fellows stand or
Fall down on their knees.
Then they swarm around me,
hive of honey bees.
I say, It's the fire in my eyes,
And the flash of my teeth,
The swing of my waist,
And the joy in my feet.
I'm a woman
Phenomenally.
Phenomenal woman,
That's me.

Men themselves have wondered
What they see in me.
They try so much
But they can't touch
My inner mystery.
When I try to show them,
They say they still can't see.
I say, It's in the arch of my back,
The sun of my smile,
The ride of my breasts,
The grace of my style.
I'm a woman
Phenomenally.
Phenomenal woman,
That's me.

Now you understand
Just why my head's not bowed.
I don't shout or jump about
Or have to talk real loud.
When you see me passing,
It ought to make you proud.
I say, It's in the click of my heels,
The bend of my hair,
the palm of my hand,
The need for my care.
'Cause I'm a woman
Phenomenally.
Phenomenal woman,
That's me

There is no great achievement that is not the result of patience, working, and waiting.
~Josiah Holland

They can conquer who believe they can.
~Ralph Waldo Emerson

When one man dies, one chapter is not torn out of the book, but translated into a better language.
~John Donne

My message to you is:
Be courageous!!
Be as brave as your fathers before you.
Have faith. Go forward.
~Thomas Edison

Dance like nobody is watching,
Love like you've never been hurt,
Work like you're not being paid.
~Anonymous

All things are possible to one who
believes.
~St. Bernard of Clairvaux

Why is it that what you hear is never
quite as interesting as what you
overhear?
~Zig Ziglar

Those who do not know how to weep
with their whole heart don't know
how to laugh either
~Golda Meir

Stephen Covey, the author of *The Seven Habits of Highly Effective People*, asks his audiences this simple question, **"How many believe that the vast majority of the people in your organization possesses far more creativity, resourcefulness, ingenuity, intelligence and talent than their job requires or even allows?"** Astonishing, in his unscientific study across the world, over 95% of people agree with this question. Do you agree or disagree? We live in a land of freedom and choices, why not create opportunities for ourselves today? More importantly, if you agree, then what are you going to do about it?

The man who does not read good books has no advantage over the man who cannot read them.
~Mark Twain

I have learned many things from my teacher; I have learned many things from my friends; and I have learned even more from my students.
~The Talmud

If the day and the night are such that you greet them with joy, and life emits a fragrance like flowers and sweet-scented herbs, it is more elastic, more starry, more immortal, that is your success.
~Henry David Thoreau

There's a world of difference between truth and facts. Facts can obscure truth.
~Maya Angelou

If you want to conquer fear,
don't think about yourself. Try
to help others, and your fears
will vanish.
~Dale Carnegie

Success is getting what you
want. Happiness is wanting
what you get.
~Carl Trumball Hayden

Life is like an ice cream cone,
you have to lick it one day at a
time.
~Charlie Brown

The secret of happiness is to admire
without desiring.

~F.H. Bradley

You can't wait for inspiration.
You have to go after it with a
club.
~Jack London

Your reputation is in the hands of
others. That's what a reputation
is. You can't control that. The
only thing you can control is your
character.
~Dr. Wayne W. Dyer

Keep away from people who try
to belittle your ambitions. Small
people always do that, but the
really great make you feel that
you, too can be great.
~Mark Twain

Why are mission statements so important, you might ask? Mission statements make you clarify your beliefs. Do not limit yourself, borrow ideas from the winning masters; how have others reached where you want to go? These forces enable you to move forward and create the compelling future that makes you "you." As the famed artist Edgar Degas explained, "It is all very well to copy what you see, but it is better to draw what you see in your mind … Then your memory and your imagination are freed from the tyranny imposed by nature."

The ability to accomplish your life's dreams is the ability to focus. Ask yourself these questions:

What are my beliefs; what do I stand for?

What is my vision of the future?

What do I want to accomplish?

What is my creed, value, or life's

philosophy?

~ABC Vision

Take a moment and develop this into your personal mission statement.

My mission statement is:

Take your mission statement and memorize it; it should be your mantra and remind you of what you stand for every day in a positive way.

The greater danger
for most of us
is not that our aim is
too high
and we miss it,
but that it is
too low
and we reach it.
~Michelangelo

Show your true colors.
Mine is yellow.
~Big Bird

The future belongs to those who
believe in the beauty of their
dreams.
~Eleanor Roosevelt

Blaming someone else is
a favorite excuse.
~Unknown

THREE

C is for Commitment

The stars are at your fingertips and the world has always been yours. So reach out for your better world today because the world awaits the missing YOU.

~Richard A. Oden
www.alexander-atta.com

U p to this point in the book, you have learned why you need to have a good attitude and be aware of your beliefs. The next phase is to develop the commitment to stay the course. Life is a marathon, not a sprint. You have to stick it out through the bad times as well as the good. No one said living your dreams was going to be easy. It is tough to do so, but so are you. According to Robert Schuller, "Tough times never last but tough people do." Believe in yourself by sticking to your commitment. This will help you focus and enable you to determine how you will achieve your goal. Modern psychological research has concluded that the focus determines the outcome. With continual change, clear vision, and being able to continue the journey, commitment will surely become a part of your psyche. If you have a goal make it happen! Condition yourself that failure is impossible.

I have a dream.
~Dr. Martin Luther King, Jr.

The secret of unleashing your true power is setting goals that are exciting enought that they truly inspire your creativity and ignite your passion.
~Anthony Robbins

It is better to be prepared for an opportunity and not have one, than to have an opportunity and not be prepared.
~Whitney Young

Each day I affirm: All my experiences are stepping stones to my greater good.
~Unknown

Everything you do is a "thought" acted upon and set into motion. No matter how small the thought may seem, it will ultimately have an affect on your life. To create the life that you want to lead, you must have a vision of this life.

This vision will give you POWER!! Yes, POWER!! It is the ultimate force of the universe; from being in a position of power and strength, your decisions will allow you to conquer the mountains ahead.

You must believe in yourself before anyone else will.

Tony Robbins outlines four steps in developing good goals. First know your outcome. Then decide and take action, followed by knowing what you are getting. Finally notice if what you are doing is working and if not, change your approach.

The Optimist Creed
Promise Yourself

To be so strong that nothing can disturb your peace of mind.

To talk health, happiness, and prosperity to every person you meet.

To make all your friends feel that there is something in them.

To look at the sunny side of everything and make your optimism come true.

To think only the best, to work only for the best and expect only the best.

To be just as enthusiastic about the success of others as you are about your own.

To forget the mistakes of the past and press on to the greater achievements of the future.

To wear a cheerful countenance at all times and give every living creature you meet a smile.

To give so much time to the improvement of yourself that you have no time to criticize others.

To be too large for worry, too noble for anger, too strong for fear, and too happy to permit the presence of trouble.

Fear is the dark room where negatives are developed.
~Zig Ziglar

About ninety percent of the things in our lives are right and about ten percent are wrong. If we want to be happy, all we have to do is to concentrate on the ninety percent that are right and ignore the ten percent that are wrong. If we want to be worried and bitter and have stomach ulcers, all we have to do is to concentrate on the ten percent that are wrong and ignore the ninety percent that are glorious.
~Dale Carnegie

A lot of people are waiting for Martin Luther King or Mahatma Gandhi to come back — but they are gone. We are it. It is up to us. It is up to you.
~Marian Wright Edelman

Civitan Creed

I AM CIVITAN: as old as life, as young as the rainbow, as endless as time.

MY HANDS do the work of the world and reach out in service to others.

MY EARS hear the cry of children and the call throughout the world for peace, guidance, progress and unity.

MY EYES search for others to join in fellowship and service of Civitan.

MY MOUTH utters the call to daily duty and speaks prayers in every tongue.

MY MIND teaches me respect for law and the flag of my country.

MY HEART beats for every friend, bleeds for every injury to humanity and throbs with joy at every triumph of truth.

MY SOUL knows no fear but its own unworthiness.

MY HOPE is for a better world through Civitan.

MY MOTTO: builders of good citizenship.

MY BELIEF: do unto others as you would have them do unto you.

MY PLEDGE: to practice the golden rule and to build upon it a better and nobler citizenship.

The ultimate measure of a man is not where he stands in the moment of comfort and convenience, but where he stands at times of challenge and controversy.
~Martin Luther King, Jr.

We train very hard- but it seemed that every time we were beginning to form up into teams, we would be reorganized. I was to learn later in life that we tend to meet any new situation by reorganizing; and a wonderful method it can be for creating the illusion of progress while producing confusion, inefficiency, and demoralization.
~Caius Petronius, 60 AD

There are no victories at bargain prices.
~Zig Ziglar

The big shots are only the little shots who keep on shooting.
~Christopher Morle

Success is.... doing the very best you can, every chance you get with what you have for a purpose that is bigger than you are and that will outlive you.
~Dr. Dwight "Ike" Reighard

LIONS CLUBS

Mission Statement
To create and foster a spirit of understanding among all people for humanitarian needs by providing voluntary services through community involvement and international cooperation.

Lions International Objectives

1. **To Create** and foster a spirit of understanding among the peoples of the world.

2. **To Promote** the principle of good government and good citizenship.

3. **To Take** an active interest in the civic, cultural, social and moral welfare of the community.

4. **To Unite** the clubs in the bonds of friendship, good fellowship and mutual understanding.

5. **To Provide** a forum for the open discussion of all matters of public interest; provided, however, that partisan politics and sectarian religion shall not be debated by club members.

6. **To Encourage** service-minded people to serve their community without personal financial reward, and to encourage efficiency and promote high ethical standards in commerce, industry, professions, public works and private endeavors.

We Serve

Action may not always bring happiness; but
there is no happiness without action.
~Benjamin Disraeli

Five Lessons For Life

1. Keep your Word and your commitments.
2. Don't look for favors- count on earning them.
3. Watch out for success- it can be more
    dangerous than failure.
4. Do what you say, say what you mean and be
    what you seem.
5. Open the envelope of your soul to discern
    God's orders hidden there.
        ~Marian Wright Edelman

The Future never just happened – it was created.
~Will Durant

Our fatigue is often caused not by work, but by
worry, frustration and resentment.
 ~Dale Carnegie

What we call the secret of happiness is no more
a secret than our willingness to choose life.
~Leo Buscaglia

GOALS

Develop a strategy to live the life YOU want to lead!

Write down your dreams today.

~ Physical Goals

~ Spiritual Goals

~ Personal Goals

~ Professional Goals

~ Financial Goals

If you really want to do something, you'll find a way. If you don't, you'll find an excuse.
~Eleanor Roosevelt

You create your own happiness in life, because you have the power to make choices and decisions. You can choose to be happy or dwell on the negative aspects in your life... the choice is yours.
~Unknown

He knows not his own strength who has not met adversity.
~Ben Johnson

Doubt is the beginning, not the end of wisdom.
~George Iles

30 DAY CHALLENGE

For the next 30 days focus on one thing that would change your life's direction and create the life that you envision. Look at this statement in the morning, noon, and night.

Concentrate all your thoughts upon the work on hand. The sun's rays do not burn until brought to a focus.
~Alexander Graham Bell

Flaming enthusiasm, backed by horse sense and persistence, is the quality that most frequently makes for success.
~Dale Carnegie

When I want to consider a particular problem, I open a certain drawer. When I have settled the matter in my mind, I close that drawer and open another. When I desire to sleep, I close all the drawers.

~Napoleon

Ambigious commitment produces mediocre results.
~Harvey Mackay

Actually, I'm an overnight success. But it took twenty years.
~ Monty Hall

In goal setting, we often tend to focus on the big goals. What really gets us closer to those big goals are the little goals that move us in that direction. A journey of a thousand miles begins with one step. Take a moment and write down 5 goals you will accomplish today!

1.

2.

3.

4.

5.

Life may not be the party we hoped for, but while we are here we might as well dance.
~Unknown

Even a clock that is not going is right twice a day.
~Polish proverb

To plan for a year, plant wheat.
To plan for ten years, plant a tree.
To plan a lifetime, develop a human mind.
~Chinese proverb

Very few people do anything creative after the age of thirty five. The reason is that very few people do anything creative before the age of thirty five.
~Joel Hildebrand

Nostalgia isn't what it used to be.
~Unknown

I like the man who bubbles over with enthusiasm. Better be a geyser than a mud puddle.
~John G. Shedd

FOUR

LEADERSHIP

Don't stand in line and follow the leader.
Make a new one and become the leader.
~Trey Ragsdale
www.purepolitics.com

In order to apply the lessons learned within the ABC model, there needs to be leadership. Leadership is one of those intangible conceptual ideals in which all individuals and organizations need in order to ensure survival. The concept of leadership continues to elude us, constantly reemerging in one form or another. The quotes found within this chapter reflect an attempt to define the ideal of leadership.

To whom much is given, much is expected.
~Leadership Cobb Class 2003

Our framework of leadership is that all of us are leaders. We all decided our fate by our actions. Once we realize that we have the potential to "awaken the leader" within, we need to understand the role of a leader. It is more than simply commanding orders, it is a responsibility to get things done. Leaders should serve as role models and empower individuals that will create a learning and creative environment. Leaders should also be guided by a set of ethical principles in determining the course of action. Theses valid components of leadership can change a world of despair towards a world of opportunity. Yes, you are a leader, now take the mantle of responsibility and move forward.

The most explored topic within organizations is leadership. Defining, developing, and becoming a leader is not an exact science. How do we determine effective leadership? Is it power? Results? or simply a means to an end? All these could be correctly used to understand leadership. Begin your journey by awakening the leader within.

A true leader inspires others to lead themselves.
~Ari D. Kaplan

A real leader spends his time fixing the problem instead of finding the blame.
~Tony Pearce

A leader is a dealer in hope.
~Napolean

The best way to have a good idea is to have lots of ideas.
~Dr. Linus Pauling

Every generation needs a new revolution.
~Thomas Jefferson

Traits found within effective
organizations.

L- Leadership- develop
leaders at all levels.

E- Environment- create a
nurturing and learning
organization.

A- Action- decisions are made
and implemented.

D- Diversity- everybody brings
treasures to the organization.

E- Expectations- establish
outrageous ambitious goals
for your organization.

R- Results- what do you do
and how well do you do it?

~Wilson L. Triviño, Ph.D.

I not only use all the brains I have,
but all I can borrow.
~Woodrow Wilson

Don't wait for your ship to come in,
swim out to it.
~Unknown

Keep the main thing the main thing.
~David Cottrell

Leaders grow; they are not made.
~Peter Drucker

I am a leader by default, only because
nature does not allow a vacuum.
~Bishop Desmond Tutu

Lead with Purpose.
~Leadership Cobb Class 2004

FIVE

PRESIDENTIAL WISDOM

It CAN be done.
~Ronald Reagan

Tact: the ability to describe others as they see themselves:
~Abraham Lincoln

Leadership is the ability to persuade other to do what you want them to do because they want to do it.
~Dwight D. Eisenhower

Surround yourself with the best people you can find, delegate authority, and don't interfere as long as the policy you've decided upon is being carried out.
~Ronald Reagan

Too often my party has confused the need for limited government with a disdain for government itself.
~George H. W. Bush

As a presidential scholars, we have a keen interest in sharing the wisdom from our nation's chief executives. The men that have held this office are extraordinary individuals. Their experience is like no other.

This chapter contains some of our favorite Presidential quotes.

War may sometimes be a necessary evil. But no matter how necessary, it is always an evil, never a good. We will not learn how to live together in peace by killing each other's children.

~ Jimmy Carter

When angry, count ten before you speak; if very angry, one hundred.

~Thomas Jefferson

Politics is not a bad profession. If you succeed there are many rewards, if you disgrace yourself you can always write a book.
~Ronald Reagan

It's a recession when you neighbor loses his job; it's a depression when you lose your own.
~Harry Truman

Mothers all want their sons to grow up to be president but they don't want them to become politicians in the process
~John F. Kennedy

Let's roll.
~George W. Bush

I want a one-armed economist so that the guy could never make a statement and then say 'on the other hand…'
~Harry Truman

Blessed are the young, for they shall inherit the National Debt.
~Herbert Hoover

We all tend to rise or fall together.
~Theodore Roosevelt

One man with courage makes a majority.
~ Andrew Jackson

The dreams of today are the realities of tomorrow.
~Franklin Delano Roosevelt

From the *United States Declaration of Independence*

When in the course of human events, it becomes necessary
for one people to dissolve the political bands which have
connected them with another, and to assume among the
powers of the earth, the separate and equal station to which
the Laws of Nature and of Nature's God entitle them, a
decent respect to the opinions of mankind requires that they
should declare the causes which impel them to the
separation.

We hold these truths to be self-evident, that all men are
created equal, that they are endowed by their Creator with
certain unalienable Rights, that among these are Life,
Liberty and the pursuit of Happiness. —That to secure
these rights, Governments are instituted among Men,
deriving their just powers from the consent of the governed,
—That whenever any Form of Government becomes
destructive of these ends, it is the Right of the People to
alter or to abolish it, and to institute new Government, laying
its foundation on such principles and organizing its powers
in such form, as to them shall seem most likely to effect their
Safety and Happiness.

Preamble to the

Constitution of the United States of America

We the people of the United States, in order to form a more
perfect union, establish justice, insure domestic tranquility,
provide for the common defense, promote the general
welfare, and secure the blessings of liberty to ourselves and
our posterity, do ordain and establish this Constitution for
the United States of America.

SIX

HUMOR

I hate quotations.
~Ralph Walso Emerson

Few women admit their age, few men act theirs.
~Unknown

Accept that some days you're the pigeon, and some days you're the statue.
~Scott Adams

Too bad all the people who know how to run the country are busy driving taxi cabs and cutting hair.
~George Burns

I love the opera... You just can't sleep that well at home.
~Dennis Miller

Finally! The last and most important chapter. You can be the most positive individual but if you can not find the humor in life's experiences you can not enjoy the journey. The quotes in this chapter will make you smile.

Life for all its incompleteness is rather fun, sometimes.
~Sir Winston Churchill

He loves his chickens!
~Papi

If you had everything, where would you put it?
~Unknown

I never forget a face, but in your case I'll make an exception.
~Groucho Marx

I failed to make the chess team because of my height.
~Woody Allen

A verbal contract isn't worth the paper it's written on.
~Samuel Goldwyn

I always arrive late at the office, but I make up for it by leaving early.
~Charles Lamb

True terror is to wake up one morning and discover that your high school class is running the country.
~Kurt Vonnegut

I can't understand why I flunked American history. When I was a kid there was so little of it.
~George Burns

I'll never learn how to spell. The teacher keeps changing the words.
~Henny Youngman

The teacher told my kid, "An apple a day keeps the doctor away." My kid asked, "What do you got for cops?"
~Rodney Dangerfield

You have to accept whatever comes,
and the only important question is
that you meet it with courage
and the best you have to give.
~Unknown

There is something yet to do.
We must grow.
We must continue to set great
purposeful goals.
We must plan our future and think
positively about it.
~Eleanor Roosevelt

Far away there in the sunshine are
my highest aspirations. I may not
reach them, but I can look up and see
their beauty, believe in them, and try
to follow where they lead.
~Louisa May Alcott

SEVEN

FINAL THOUGHTS

ONE.

~C. David Triviño

86

We live in a world of hope and excitement. Never before have so many opportunities been available to so many. With the modern age upon us, our potential is limitless.

The quotes in this book are a very small part of our favorite passages. We have worked toward allowing these ideas to generate the momentum that is needed to move toward a successful life that centers around on focusing on your individual Attitude, Beliefs, and Commitment.

As you complete this book, I encourage that you take a moment and reflect on your life as it exist today. Take a look into the state in which you find yourself and spell out where you would like to go. Without establishing a path, then how do you know where you want to go? In this life journey, we are writing a story. If you are not happy with what life has to offer, then change it.

Take a moment and decide that today you will live the life you want to lead!

Today is the best day to begin the path for a better tomorrow.

LIVE LIFE WITH PASSION!

THE FINAL WORD

If you have a penny and we have a penny and we exchange pennies, you still have one cent and we have one cent.

But if you have an idea and we have an idea and we exchange ideas, you now have two ideas and we have two ideas.

Thank you for taking the time in reading *Remember Your ABC Lite*. Please pass along this book to your friends and family to spread the knowledge.

We would also ask that you share with me your comments on this book and any personal stories on how you may have reached your own success.

Continue to live life with passion and live the life YOU want to lead!

Wilson Triviño, Ph.D.
C. David Triviño
July 2003

Mail these comments to:

ABC Vision
379 Pat Mell Road
Suite 123
Marietta, GA 30060

Or email:
success@abcvision.us

www.abcvision.us

Auburn University

"WAR EAGLE"

War...Eagle, fly down the field,
Ever to conquer, never to yield.
War...Eagle fearless and true.
Fight on, you orange and blue.
Go! Go! Go!
On to vic'try, strike up the band,
Give 'em hell, give 'em hell.
Stand up and yell, Hey!
War...Eagle,
win for Auburn,
Power of Dixie Land!

Georgia Tech
"Ramblin' Wreck"

I'm a Ramblin' Wreck From Georgia Tech
and a hell of an engineer.A helluva helluva
helluva helluva helluvan engineer.Like all
the jolly good fellows, I drink my whiskey
clear,I'm a Ramblin' Wreck from Georgia
Tech and a hell of an engineer.

Oh, If I had a daughter, sir, I'd dress her in
White and Gold.And put her on the campus
to cheer the brave and bold.And if I had a
son, sir, I'll tell you what he'd do,He would
yell "TO HELL WITH GEORGIA" like his
daddy used to do.

I wish I had a barrel of rum and sugar three
thousand pounds,A college bell to put it in,
and a clapper to stir it round.I'd drink to all
the good fellows who come from far and
near,I'm a ramblin, gamblin' hell of an
engineer, Hey!

References

Carnegie, Dale. 1984. *How to Stop Worrying and Start Living.* New York, NY: Simon and Schuster.

Cleland, Max. 2000. *Strong at the Broken Places.* Marietta, GA: Longstreet Press.

Cleland, Max. 1999. *Going for The Max: 12 Principles for Living Life to the Fullest.* Nashville, TN: Broadman & Holman Publisher.

Cottrell, David. 2002. *Monday Morning Leadership.* Dallas, TX: Cornerstone Leadership Institute.

Covey, Stephen R. 1990. *The 7 Habits of Highly Effective People.* New York, NY: Simon & Schuster, Inc.

Dali, Lama and Howard C. Cutler. 1998. *The Art of Happiness.* New York, NY: Penguin Books.

Dyer, Wayne W. 1998. *Wisdom of the Ages.* New York, NY: Harper Collins Books.

Larkin, Willie D. 1998. *Choose Not To be Average Strive to be Great!.* Auburn, AL:Cotton Patch Publishing.

Purkey, William W. and Betty L. Siegel. 2002. *Becoming An Invitational Leader: A New Approach to Professional and Personal Success.* Atlanta, GA: Brumby Holdings, Inc.

Reighard, Dwight. 1998. *Discover Your North Star: Charting Your Course For Success & Significance.* Atlanta, Georgia: Quantum Lead Publishing.

Robbins, Anthony. 1991. *Awaken the Giant Within.* New York, NY: Fireside Books.

Schuller, Robert H. 1987. *The Be (Happy) Attitudes.* Irving, TX: Bantam Books.

Ziglar, Zig. 1999. *Something Else to Smile About.* Nashville, TN: Thomas Nelson, Inc.

91

Wilson Triviño, Ph.D.
Biography

Dr. Wilson Triviño is a speaker and writer for ABC Vision, a consulting firm that centers on individuals and organizations as they deal with leadership, change, and diversity. His experience within the business, political, and educational fields allows him to interact with today's world achievers and share their insights with his audiences.

Wilson was the first Latino to receive a doctorate in Public Policy and Public Administration from Auburn University in Auburn, Alabama. He holds a Masters of Public Administration from Auburn University and a Bachelor of Arts from Kennesaw State University.

Wilson's first book, *Remember Your ABCs*, centers on how you can become a success by focusing on your Attitude, Beliefs, and Commitment.

Wilson is an active member of the Latino Institute For Excellence (LIFE), a nonpartisan and not-for-profit advocacy group seeking to develop leaders within the Latino community through education, entrepreneurship, and economic development. Through these efforts, the current Bush Administration has identified Wilson as a leader within the Latino community which is the single fastest growing demographic group in the nation.

As a distinguished Presidential scholar, Wilson was invited to participate in the 100 year celebration of the West Wing. This symposium brought together a powerful chorus to sing the West Wing's praises including such notables as Vice President Dick Cheney, Mike McCurry, former Clinton Press Secretary, and other inhabitants of this powerful political real estate. The highlight of the event was a private tour and discussion of the White House led by President Bush and the First Lady.

Wilson's doctoral dissertation focused on organizational change within the Social Security Administration. This research led former President Bill Clinton to recognize Wilson as one of the nation's leading experts on Social Security at a White House conference. Wilson has also served as a technical resource for the United States Congress through his briefings he has given to congressmen and congressional staff on Social Security issues.

While completing his graduate studies at Auburn University, Wilson taught in the Department of Political Science. He also works with bi-partisan public advocacy groups such as the National Committee to Preserve Social Security and Medicare and the Concord Coalition.

Wilson is also a contributing writer to the online political magazine, www.purepolitics.com , reporting on current political topics.

Wilson has appeared on several television programs which include appearances on CNN, C-Span, Georgia Public Television, Cafe Central TV, and Channel 12, People's TV.

Early in his career Wilson worked with the Georgia House of Representatives, Georgia's Secretary of State, and as an executive assistant to the Southern Regional Commissioner of the Social Security Administration in Atlanta, Georgia. He has also been active as a strategist in federal, state, and local political campaigns.

C. David Triviño
Biography

David Triviño is a businessman and entrepreneur who currently manages, Lubin's Transmission, the 25 year old family automotive business in Marietta, Georgia. David holds a Master of Business Administration (MBA) and a Bachelor of Science (BS) in Management degree from Georgia Tech. He lectures on leadership and diversity within the world of business.

David serves on the board of director of the Latino Institute For Excellence (LIFE), a nonpartisan and not-for-profit advocacy group seeking to develop leaders within the Latino community through education, entrepreneurship, and economic development.

David is a graduate of the Cobb County Chamber of Commerce's 2003 leadership Cobb Class as well as an avid salsa dancer. He resides in Marietta, Georgia.

To schedule a dynamic speaker at your organization's next event, call 404.918.1774 or for more information visit www.abcvision.us.

ABC Vision
Suite 123
379 Pat Mell Road
Marietta, Georgia 30060
404.918.1774 fax 770.426.9977
e-mail: success@abcvision.us

Give the gift of ideas!

BOOK ORDER FORM

$15.00 ~~ *Remember Your ABCs:*
A simple guide on how to become a success
and live the life YOU want to lead!
Item number 100

$10.00 ~~*Remember YOU ABCs Lite:*
Quotes and ideas that will empower you to
to live the life YOU want to lead!
Item Number 200

$5 per book for Shipping & Handling within the
USA or call for bulk orders

ITEM #	Unit Cost	Quantity	Total
_____	_____	_____	_____
_____	_____	_____	_____

TOTAL ENCLOSED _____

Name:_____

Address:_____

City:_____ State:__ Zip:_____

Phone: _____

Make check payable to **ABC Vision**

Send your order form to:
ABC Vision
Suite 123
Marietta, GA 30060
Fax 770.426.9977 or 404.918.1774

If you are a writer and would like to get your book published contact:

T4 Group

www.t4group.us
ideas@t4group.us
t4group@hotmail.com

Success is living the life
YOU want to lead!
~Dr. Wilson Triviño
www.abcvision.us

Today is the tomorrow that you
worried about yesterday!
~Unknown

The future is ours to do.
~Windsor Jordan
Mary Jordan Catering Service, Inc.

Strive to do what you love and love
what you do.
~Kelly Conn

The great doors of opportunity swing
on the tiny hinges of obedience.
~Dr. Dwight "Ike" Reighard

Live your dreams today!